Penance

by
David Gregg
*Information Secretary of the Board for Mission and Unity, General Synod
of the Church of England*

GROVE BOOKS
BRAMCOTE NOTTS.

CONTENTS

		Page
	Introduction	3
1.	Why 'Penance'?	4
2.	The Theology of 'Penance'	7
3.	Pastoral 'Penance'	14
4.	Liturgical 'Penance'	18
5.	'Matters Arising'	23

Copyright David Gregg 1977

EXPLANATORY NOTE

This booklet is produced in the author's personal capacity and is not an official production of the Board for Mission and Unity.

First Impression August 1977

ISSN 0305 3067

ISBN 0 905422 19 8

INTRODUCTION

It is with some apprehension that I embark on the Grove Booklet on Ministry and Worship with the shortest title so far ventured—'Penance'. Not least because such a title may arouse in readers hopes and expectations which I cannot hope to fulfil in the space of 24 pages. But perhaps, if I could explain my own motives for this essay, its own modest pretensions will be allowed to play their part in the judgment placed upon it.

I should like to try and convey something of how it feels to be a twentieth-century evangelical Anglican slowly waking up to a realization that (as with his understanding of the eucharist, fasting, healing, exorcism, the corporate nature of the Church, the use of silence and meditation, or the scope for drama and dancing in worship, to name but a few) here is an area of Christian experience on which he has been gravely 'missing out'. As this will therefore involve an exploration of neglected terrain, I must ask for some indulgence from those for whom this will contain much that is obvious and much that may seem naive. I am reminded of the reaction of the Zambians when asked to issue a stamp to commemorate the centenary of David Livingstone's 'discovery' of the Victoria Falls. They replied, 'Oh, no! We knew it was there already!'

My limited ambition is only to open up the subject for those in today's church who (like myself) have not really perhaps been taking this as seriously as they ought. When one discovers the central importance placed on this aspect of the Christian faith by Roman Catholic, Orthodox, Reformation, Puritan and Tractarian traditions, one can only marvel at its relative neglect in contemporary Anglican life (with the honorable exception of the anglo-catholic element). If I can bring the range of topics covered by this title more to the surface, and help to kindle an awareness of the centrality and importance of this theme in the whole range of the matters that are covered by this series on Ministry and Worship, I will be more than content.

My own immediate interest was kindled by reading Nicholas Sagovsky's booklet *Modern Roman Catholic Worship: Baptism and Penance.*[1] For me this opened up a rich vein of theology which has proved most edifying and stimulating. I am most grateful to my colleagues in the Group for Renewal of Worship for encouraging me to pursue some of the leads that are given there, and they were eventually persuaded that a more general treatment of the subject was a conspicuous omission from this series. This booklet is the result, however, of my own meanderings, though I hope that the disciplining of my thinking which I owe to the group will be evident from time to time. Some (brief) repetition of certain points made in Booklet 43 will be inevitable, but it is my hope that this present booklet may prove to be a general guide to a whole diamond-mine, in which the subject of that booklet forms a particular gallery.

David Gregg
July 1977

[1] Grove Booklet no. 43 (April 1976)

1. WHY 'PENANCE'?

Universality

If we allow our minds to wander over the whole range of human history and contemporary experience, we become aware of certain 'universals' that are common to humankind. And in one such 'universal' we find a phenomenom which runs right through from the time of the oldest remains of ritual sacrifice to the newest rituals, of self-criticism and 'struggle' and confession, that typify the most modern 'religions' of the masses, Marxism and Maoism. The 'universal' is the sense of alienation, which comes from departing from established and required 'norms' of behaviour, and the phenomenon is the provision of certain ritualistic means to overcome this and to re-establish harmony either with the community or with the gods, or both. So, between the extremes just mentioned, across the centuries and across the globe, we could catalogue, for instance, the elaborate ceremonies of the Animists to appease their spirits; the significance for Hindus of bathing in the Ganges and dying on its banks; the Buddhist quest for *Nirvana* through the Middle Way and the eightfold-path; the *Yom Kippur* of Judaism and the *O-harai* of Shinto; the Vedic confessions to the god Varuna; the five pillars of Islam; the ritual 'ordeals' of North American Indians, and even the traditional methods of modern Trades Unions for dealing with wayward members! We have here, then, a commonplace of human life. It is inconceivable that Christianity alone would fail to address it.

Centrality

The context in which the Christian will meet the phenomenon of these 'rituals of reconciliation' is the absolute, basic, and fundamental one of the holiness of God, the personal responsibility and answerability of man, the universality of sin, the experience of guilt, and the need for reconciliation and forgiveness. But Christianity has here its own uniqueness. As Sir Norman Anderson has put it:

> 'Christianity brings the "good news" of a salvation which is wholly God-provided: man can do nothing to earn it or achieve it, but can only accept it as a gift. Where every other religion teaches what man must *do,* Christianity alone tells what God has *done.*'[1]

It will be important to keep our eyes steadfastly on this basic fact as we grapple with the issues ahead.

There can be no doubt about the importance of our subject in the Christian scheme of things.[2] How salutary that the Devil's chief function, epitomized in his name of Satan, is to be the 'Accuser of the Brethren' (Rev. 12.10; cf. Job 1 and 2). What a wealth of truth about the interdependence of good and evil is enshrined in the concept of the Evil One as a foil for God's great grace.

---

[1] *The World's Religions* (IVF, London, 1955) p.195.
[2] Compare the quaint opening words of the Homily of Repentance:
> 'There is nothing that the Holy Ghost doth so much labour in all the Scriptures to beat into men's heads, as repentance, amendment of life, and speedy returning unto the Lord God of hosts.'

(And it proceeds to occupy 25 pages of my edition with citations to prove it!).

WHY 'PENANCE'?

But has the whole subject of 'Penance' to do with the dark and gloomy and negative side of our faith? Surely not![1] The realization that penance is an indispensable prelude to the experience of the joy of the gospel is basic to the stories of David (Ps. 51.8-12), of Zaccheus (Lk. 19.6) and of the Prodigal Son (Lk. 15.24). It is born out in the testimony of Christians down the ages. It is another aspect of our subject of which we must take care not to lose sight.

Particularity

Why then use the word 'Penance'? What is implied by it? It derives from a whole area of time-honoured Catholic theologizing under the title 'The Sacrament of Penance' (with all the negative connotations *that* may arouse in Protestant breasts). But if we define its use here, the choice will appear not only less exceptionable, but even somewhat unavoidable. The main reason is that no other word that I am aware of will do!

What we want is a liturgical word that will embrace the whole spectrum of Christian practice that relates to dealing with sin in the life of the believer. This obviously starts with baptism, which is the initial sacramental means of dealing with sin, but we shall need to see baptism as only the *beginning* of the penitential life. We must avoid, on the one hand, the error of viewing baptism as *the* once-for-all, and only means of dealing with sin, (which entails putting off baptism till the last possible moment in life, as the fourth-century church did), and, on the other hand, viewing 'penance' as being a sort of once-for-all 'back-stop' to be used only in exceptional circumstances for extremely serious post-baptismal sin (which entails creatng a separate 'Order of penitents', with life-long disabilities attached to it, and a putting-off of *Penance* till the eve of death, such as arose in the third-century church and continued into the Middle Ages). Article XVI succinctly sets the bounds of our present concern:

> 'After we have received the Holy Ghost, we may depart from grace given, and fall into sin, and by the grace of God we may rise again, and amend our lives. And therefore they are to be condemned, which say, they can no more sin as long as they live here, or deny the place of forgiveness to such as truly repent.'

What we need is a word that covers objectively the whole matter dealt with in this Article, and in 'Penance' we have just such a word ready to hand. The word was given its classical definition by Thomas Aquinas, and was 'canonized' by the Council of Trent, as covering four main categories: Contrition—Confession—Satisfaction—Absolution.[2]

---

[1] Basilea Schlink offers a timely and invaluable corrective:
'Long ago John the Baptist cried out, "Repent, the Kingdom of Heaven is at hand." Is that not the very basis of the Gospel, the Good News? Repentance—the gate to heaven! Repentance—the gate to the very heart of the Father! Yes, repentance makes us joyful and blissful. It brings us home to the heart of the Father; it brings us all the way to heaven.' (*Repentance—the Joy-filled Life* (Lakeland, London, 1969) p.13).

[2] cf. J. D. Crichton *The Ministry of Reconciliation* (London, Chapman, 1974) p.20.

PENANCE

That these *exactly* coincide with classical (and scripturally respectable) Anglican analysis of the subject in hand is very neatly borne out in the above-mentioned 32nd Homily:

> 'Now there be four parts of repentance, which, being set together may be likened to an easy and short ladder . . .
>
> The first is contrition of the heart. . . .
>
> The second is, an unfeigned confession and acknowledgement of our sins unto God, . . .
>
> The third part of repentance is faith, whereby we do apprehend and take hold upon the promises of God, touching the free pardon and forgiveness of our sins: which promises are sealed up unto us, with the death and blood-shedding of his Son Jesus Christ. . . .
>
> The fourth is, an amendment of life, or a new life, in bringing forth fruits worthy of repentance.'

The alert reader will notice two things. The Catholic order has 'Satisfaction' before 'Absolution' (this is because the first three relate to the 'acts of the penitent'); and the Homily uses the term 'repentance' rather than 'penance'. 'Repentance' is arguably inappropriate for our purpose because it is a broadly *moral* term, rather than a liturgical one.[1] 'Penance' is used as basically a liturgical word (including any specific acts which are appropriate)[2], and, on this understanding, we will employ it as our generic term.[3]

Finally, may we return briefly to our opening observation about this subject relating to a basic 'universal' of our humanity. Since the Christian believes that any such universal is a consequence of the way the Lord has made us, the full appropriation of all that *he* has revealed on the subject, and the implementation of *his* instructions will be paramount. We see the force of Augustine's famous dictum:

> 'You have created us for yourself, and our heart is restless until it finds repose in you.'

and it is to the biblical theology of penance that we now turn.

---

[1] For further proof that this traditional analysis really *does* do justice to the whole counsel of God on this matter, it is impressive to look closely at that *locus classicus*, Psalm 51. It is a rewarding exercise, to which we will allude at length as we go on, to see how David's own experience and awareness co-incides closely with the four facets of Penance set out above.

[2] Some uses of the word imply 'Contrition' and 'Confession' only, but this does less than justice to the moral conversion implied in the scriptural use of the term.

[3] The distinction should now be clear: 'Repentance' may be practised through the use of 'Penance'—but it may also be practised independently of it; 'Penance' when practised should involve 'Repentance', but as a liturgical act it can logically occur with an outward form but without any true 'Repentance'. (The Homily, of course, is careful to insist on the moral conversion *without* institutionalizing it in a liturgical act).

2. THE THEOLOGY OF 'PENANCE'

We will examine the theology of penance under the four traditional headings, but in the order favoured by the Homily,—contrition, confession, absolution and satisfaction. Then follow some general remarks about the essentially *corporate* nature of the theology of penance, for our primary concern is with the spiritual 'machinery' whereby the covenant community, the Church of Jesus Christ, makes provision for the restoration of the individual member of the covenant, to full fellowship again, when he or she has fallen into sin. This means that all that is generally understood by 'Covenant Theology' lies behind what is written here.

Contrition

Penance begins where Psalm 51 begins it, 'Have mercy on me, O God.' It is the place commended by Jesus in his story of the Pharisee and the tax collector, 'God, be merciful to me a sinner!' (Lk. 18.13). Is it possibly significant that both pleas for mercy use the term 'God' rather than the covenant name of 'Lord'? Certainly, one of the crucial things that is broken by unforgiven sin is the sense of intimacy and interdependence of personal relationships that the use of the personal name of God bespeaks. But, at the same time there is (explicit in the case of David and, one suspects, implicit with the tax collector) an awareness of the love and mercy of Almighty God, and, perhaps most crucial of all, a belief in his *power* to forgive (Ps. 51.1-2), which is the vital trigger to contrition. And it is made clear that contrition is the indispensable key to all the rest. Without it there can be no *genuine* confession, no effective pronouncing of absolution, no enjoyment of 'justification' (Ps. 15.17; Lk. 18.14).

The Hebrew word most characteristically used of human contrition in the Old Testament is *shub* 'to turn'. It is, as usual, a basically *physical* image, perhaps better captured by the idiom of 'about face'. It corresponds to the way God himself is said to *turn* from anger to favour and blessing, and it marks a turning *from* sin *to* God, with heart and soul and mind and strength. In the New Testament the basic imagery is more intellectual, with the characteristic word *metanoeo* meaning a radical change of mind. However, it is frequently found co-ordinated with *epistrepho*, 'to turn', and the latter is sometimes found on its own as a synonym for *metanoeo*.[1]

There are many facets to the Scriptural teaching about contrition (perhaps here we may substitute the term 'repentance' in its more limited sense) which we can only touch upon briefly. It is clear, for instance, that repentance cannot just be a mere intellectual recognition of something that is wrong. A genuine and emotional 'grief' over sin is called for as well. It is all too possible to know that one is in the wrong *without* being really 'sorry' (cf. Acts 5.1-11). But sorrowful repentance is shown to be an essential pre-requisite for faith in the gospel (Mk. 1.15; Acts 2.38). Without it, man is confirmed in his waywardness, and doomed to unending alienation from God (Lk. 13.1-5), just as in broken human relationships there can be no reconciliation until the offending party experiences and expresses

---

[1] cf. Art. 'Repentance' in the *New Bible Dictionary* (IVF, London, 1962).

sorrow for what he has done. (Mt. 18.15-22). So repentance and faith are inseparable, and that, *not* as a mere option dependent on man's own whim. Repentance is *commanded* by God. (Acts 17.30; cf. Mk. 2.17). And even the *capacity* to repent is spoken of as an act of God's gracious initiative (Acts 11.18).

All this is very obviously relevant to the *initial* turning of a human soul to God, but the context of this booklet requires discussion of its application to subsequent acts of repentance as well. Perhaps there is too strong a theoretical distinction here, for in scripture *all* repentance is conceived of not as an initial *turning* to God, as to one with whom there has existed no previous relationship at all, but as a *re*-turning to one who already has an existing relationship to the sinner, with consequent rights and obligations. The fundamental analogies of the lost sheep, the lost coin and the prodigal son amply illustrate this perspective, and even Paul's attitude to the Athenians bears it out. Of course, it is true that the first conscious returning to God will have certain features incapable of repetition (—there can only be one 'first time' for anything), but the New Testament does not allow any essential distinction to be drawn between the 'repentance' that is a constituent of the initial reconciliation, and subsequent acts which become necessary within that renewed relationship.[1]

The most we can say is that when 'repentance' *(metanoeo)* and 'turning' *(epistrepho)* occur *together* in the New Testament this usually means *initial* returning[2], but otherwise the uses of *metanoeo* are imprecise and non-specific. Contrition, then—the experience of sorrowful repentance in the heart—we take to be the spiritual reality that must be present to validate all that follows.

Confession

Psalm 51 *is* an act of confession! As 'contrition' signifies repentance in the heart, so 'confession' signifies the verbal articulation whereby the soul formulates and externalizes its inner experiences in this matter. Confession is necessarily subsequent to contrition, and it may take varying degrees of formality, from the simple cry of the Tax Collector to the most elaborate and comprehensive liturgical forms. Classically three chief types are identified: general confession, personal confession and sacramental confession.[3] It may be interesting to note in passing that a major distinguishing feature of the main Christian traditions has been the difference of emphasis here, with general confession dominating the Lutheran and Anglican traditions, personal confession the Reformed and Evangelical, and Sacramental confession the Catholic and Orthodox. It is the writer's belief, however, that these divisions are arbitrary and artificial, though all three elements have their rightful place when interwoven into the whole. So, although all three will be further alluded to, no further attempt will be made to utilize this classical analysis methodologically.

[1] Such as that enjoined upon the Church in Sardis, for instance (Rev. 3.3).
[2] And *epistrepho* on its own does usually refer to a 'one-off' experience.
[3] cf., e.g., Art. on 'Prayer' in J. G. Davies (ed.) *A Dictionary of Liturgy and Worship* (SCM 1972).

THE THEOLOGY OF 'PENANCE'

The basic biblical idea covered by 'confession' is the *acknowledgement* by the penitent of his sin. In Hebrew it is the root idea of *yadah* 'to throw, cast' which gives the hiphilic form 'to acknowledge'. It is surely noteworthy that the same verb does double duty, signifying as it does the act of *praise*—the acknowledging of God for what he is—as well as the act of *penitential confession*—the acknowledging by the sinner of what he himself is. Indeed there appears to be an intimate and mysterious connection between the two, so that real praise of God springs from a realization of the immensity of the gap that lies between the 'Holiest in the height' and the men of 'sin and shame' who have become the object of such 'generous love'. Abject humility before God is the appropriate cloak for human confession of sin, as David once again so forthrightly exemplifies (Ps. 51.3-5).

Not surprisingly perhaps, the New Testament equivalent embraces a parallel conjunction of ideas. *Homologeo* and its compounds, the public act of confessing or acknowledging, do duty both for 'confessing' Christ as Saviour and for 'confessing' sins before God and men. The basic meaning is 'to say the same thing', a reference to the act of acknowledging something to be the case, usually in agreement with others of the same mind.[1]

If the experience of 'contrition' is the *sine qua non* of our subject, the act of confession is that which gives 'contrition' objective reality and sets in train the whole process of restoration. The Prodigal in his pig-pen might well agonize in his soul, but it is his, 'Father, I have sinned against heaven and before you; I am no longer worthy to be called your son,' which contains the means to bridge the gulf between contrition and full restoration.

Absolution

This heading moves us on to the notion of forgiveness, the divine remission of sins, which marks God's side of the total transaction with which we are concerned. It is the element for which David is looking when he pleads for mercy, for the blotting out of his transgressions, for washing and for cleansing (Ps. 51.1-2). It is the gift mediated to Isaiah by the seraph, with the burning coal, and the words, 'Your guilt is taken away and your sin is forgiven' (Is. 6.7). It is the content of the healing word of Jesus to the paralytic (Mt. 9.2) and to the prostitute (Lk. 7.47).

The scriptural vocabulary of forgiveness is striking and powerful. In both Old and New Testaments the idea of 'loosing', 'letting go' and 'sending away' is fundamental, (*salach* in Hebrew, and *aphiemi* in Greek). In addition the Hebrew has *nasa'*, 'to lift, carry away', although, as we have noted already in Psalm 51, a wide variety of other analogies is invoked as well, among which ideas of 'covering', 'blotting out' etc. are prominent.[2] But every single human being knows, at some level, the experience of relief when one who has been offended frees the offender from his indebtedness and a barrier is removed, a load of anguish evaporates, a 'burden rolls away'. And surely this is the place to make the well-marked point that it is the *forgiver* who bears the cost of forgiveness, and that the one who is forgiven is entirely the beneficiary.

[1] cf. Art. 'Confession' in the *New Bible Dictionary* (IVP, London, 1962).
[2] cf. Art. 'Forgiveness' in the *New Bible Dictionary* (IVP, London, 1962).

PENANCE

In the area we are considering, the ultimate forgiver is God himself, but it is at this point in the process of penance (which we have labelled 'absolution') that the Church comes in as the instrument and agent of God's effective action, and here a particular dispute has arisen to which we must now turn. Is the role of the Church simply to *pronounce* forgiveness, or is it to *impart* forgiveness? Is the word of absolution (i.e. 'Your sins are forgiven', in some form) *performative* or merely *declaratory*? And are powers vested in *individual* ministers, or only in the Church as a whole?

The gospel passages most usually adduced in connection with these questions are Matthew 16.19 and 18.18, Luke 24.47 and John 20.23. Of these, the last three are cast in the plural, whilst only the first is in the singular. Matthew 16.19 has no necessary reference to absolution at all, but deals with the conferring of (Rabbinic?) authority to interpret the Torah. Matthew 18.18, on the other hand, clearly *is* in the context of absolution, whilst Luke 24.47 and John 20.23 have specific reference to the forgiveness of sins. It is tempting to conclude that there is no warrant in Scripture for any *individual* exercising of the ministry of absolution. It has been alleged that even Matthew 16.19 is treating Peter as *representative* of the Church as a whole! But if so, one is neatly caught in the nice irony that, in exercising its authority in respect of these very passages, the major interpretation of the Church as a whole has been that these passages *do* justify the individual exercise of the authority to absolve!

However it is John 20.23 that is surely our most important lead. There Jesus confers authority on his Church, his body, to act *for him*, as his instrument, the bearer of *his spirit*. The ministry of absolution is essentially charismatic. It is not the words themselves that achieve anything. It is the extent to which they articulate the reality of the situation in hand.[1] And, as with all such 'prophetic' signs and utterances, the word is *both* declaratory *and* performative. The dichotomy is a false one! Doubtless the function will sometimes (some would say normally) be exercised by duly ordained ministers[2], though, clearly, collective ministry in this regard may also be appropriate on occasions. But, whichever way we come at it, there is hardly any good scriptural justification for separating the performative and declaratory aspects, even if they may be logically distinguished from each other.

There must follow a broader consideration of the place of the Church at large in the theme of penance. But it is worth noting here that, when the large in the theme of Penance. it is worth noting here that, when the individual Christian is restored and absolved, the whole body benefits as well. No wonder that Psalm 51 ends as it does, with the vision of Zion blessed and rebuilt.

[1] Jesus' own ministry in this matter (e.g. to the paralytic and to the prostitute as noted above) seems to suggest the possibility of *discerning* true repentance and allowing the pronouncing of absolution *without* any overt (liturgical) 'confession' to precede it.

[2] Peter's dealings with Ananias and Sapphira (Acts 5.1-11), and Paul's pronouncement against the incestuous man (1 Cor. 5.2), both clearly show the individual minister exercising the authority to 'bind', at least!

Satisfaction

This label covers a whole area of our subject where the greatest abuses and misunderstandings have occurred. It is almost certainly because of the gross aberrations (either alleged or actual) here, that some neglect of this ministry in Protestant circles has arisen. Briefly it concerns the question of the 'price to be paid' for forgiveness, and who pays it?

On the one hand the biblical Christian will want to assert the unique significance, centrality and sufficiency of the Cross of Jesus Christ, as being the 'full, perfect, and sufficient sacrifice, oblation, and satisfaction, for the sins of the whole world.'[1] It is the cross which marks the forehead of the newly baptized. It is the cross which marks the Churches' eucharistic tables. It is the cross which marks the graves and tombs of her saints at rest. This is no place for theories of the atonement to be thrashed out, but no amount of qualification can detract from this one simple truth, that biblical Christianity has as its focus, pivot, and all-pervading theme, the cross of Jesus Christ.[2]

Such an insistence on the complete efficacy of Christ's atoning death does of course rule out the possibility of supplementing it with notions such as purgatory, indulgences, merits, and other aberrations which have historically attached themselves to the ministry of Penance.[3] It is refreshing

---

[1] I write these words looking out over the little town of Voss, in Norway. Its oldest artefact is the simple stone cross of St. Olav erected in 1023, when its population accepted Christianity. It was not the 'gentle Jesus, meek and mild' that first appealed to the hearts of these wild Vikings, but 'the courage of the Christ who chose to ascend the cross'. (T. K. Derry: *A Short History of Norway* (London 1968) p.46).

[2] I must admit to strong personal preference for the word 'propitiation' in connection with the atoning death of Christ, because it highlights the *personal* relationships involved. 'Expiation', by contrast, seems to have a rather cold, objective and juridicial ring about it. We would not, however, want to exclude other aspects of the atonement, as having *no* valid significance. In particular, the exemplary nature of Christ's death, the theme of Christ as victor, and his making available of new *life*, all commend themselves as parts (if subordinate parts) of the rich complexity of motifs that attach to the event which Christians must see as the sacred hinge of human history. Attempts to present any one interpretation as of *exclusive* validity are to be firmly resisted.

The most significant vocabulary, however, in connection with the Atonement, particularly where the connection between the Cross and human sin is concerned, seems to us to be that which attaches to 'propitiation'. So it is the Hebrew *kipper* 'to cover' (as found, for instance, in *yom kippur* 'The Day of Atonement') and the Greek *hilaskomai* 'conciliate', which chiefly express the theme of 'the removal of wrath by the offering of a gift'. (cf. Art. 'Propitiation' in the *New Bible Dictionary* (IVP, London, 1962). However unacceptable this analogy may appear to certain sophisticated intellectual Western minds, it is difficult to deny that it *is* the one that dominates the minds of the biblical writers.

[3] Even the Latin root of 'Penance'—'Poena', 'punishment'—is inappropriate. And the Vulgate rendering of *metanoeo*, i.e. 'Poenitentiam ago' (as, e.g. in Mt. 3.2, Acts 2.38, Rev. 3.3) is misleading.

PENANCE

therefore to read the following in connection with the Sacrament of Penance in a recent editorial of a leading Roman Catholic journal:

'We have to return to the Catholic teaching that forgiveness is not cheap but absolutely free, that the mercy of God is shown not in the lightness of the conditions for forgiveness but in the fact that there is forgiveness at all. We have to recognize (and this is a piece of traditional Catholicism we can usefully re-learn from our Protestant Brethren) both the seriousness of sin (and the "impossibility" of forgiveness) and the limitless compassion and unconditional forgiveness of God.'[1]

But although the biblical Christian will insist on maintaining that the death of Jesus Christ offers complete 'satisfaction' for sin (Rom. 3.19-26), he will also want to do full justice to a parallel truth that must be just as firmly adhered to, namely that true repentance requires 'amendment of life'. He will be impressed, as David was, with the idea that it is what *God* requires that matters (Ps. 51.17)—and that in Hebraic thought the *mutuality* of the covenant requires a corresponding act of the will on the part of man, in the whole transaction of 'Penance', to ensure the bringing forth of 'fruits worthy of repentance' (Lk. 3.8). In other words, the penitent also has 'a price to pay'—not to *earn* forgiveness, but to *authenticate* it! So there is a necessity for lives that match up to our repentance, if penance is to be effective and realistic (cf., e.g. Amos 5.21-24); there is the possibility of confessing God before men, and proclaiming the gospel, as a way of 'satisfying' God (Ps. 51.13, 14; cf. Jas. 5.20); there is the knowledge that love is efficacious as the fruit of repentance (Prov. 10.12).

So we come full circle. Just as Isaiah discovered the pattern of contrition and confession, absolution and satisfaction, intermingled with praise, and issuing in righteous service of the Lord (Is. 6.5, 7, 8 and 3), so too with David—the 'Penance' experience releases the soul for its true vocation of praise and service to Almighty God. (Ps. 51.15).

The Individual and the Church

Penance is essentially a 'corporate' rather than a purely 'individual' matter. We have already noted the Church's role in mediating God's forgiveness to the individual in Absolution, and that this is essentially a charismatic, rather than a merely mechanical, ministry. The *corporate* nature of penance is amply witnessed to historically, and a brief reminder of such features as the mediaeval Order of Penitents, the early Methodist 'Class system', and traditional Salvation Army practice shows the ecumenical spread of this awareness.[2] The biblical concept of putting members out

---

[1] *New Blackfriars* (March 1977) p.107.
[2] The following quotation, from a classical *Orthodox* source, further extends the scope of this:

'Concerning the Sacrament of Penance the Holy Church teaches that without it the spirit of man cannot be cleansed from the bondage of sin and of sinful pride: that he himself cannot remit his own sins (for we have only the power to condemn, not to justify ourselves), and that the Church alone has the power of justifying, for within her lives the fulness of the Spirit of Christ.'
(A. E. Khomiakov: *The Church is One* (ET, London 1968) p.34).

THE THEOLOGY OF 'PENANCE'

of fellowship and of restoring them to it bespeaks a similar emphasis on the Church, (especially in the sense of the 'local congregation',) as essentially a forgiving and reconciling fellowship. But a case-study of a remarkable modern episode, the East Africa Revival, may afford a useful illustration of this point, and a helpful transition to the practical sections with which this booklet concludes.[1]

The recent experience of the Church in East Africa is very instructive, because many thousands (or even millions) have been brought to Christian faith in recent decades through a simple emphasis on repentance and confession. The movement began in the early thirties with individuals learning to say 'sorry' *to one another* as a key to getting things right with God and with each other. An attempt to be 'Walking in the light', with a prevailing spirit of 'I feel that I have put my foot in it with you', rather than 'You have put your foot in it with me' became a foundation practice. This spread to *corporate* meetings, so that the attempt to put things right with the whole fellowship became a regular feature of the revival. The fellowship meetings became (and still are) a 'clearing-house' for putting right all sorts of personal and public matters relating to human sin. It is inherent in the African upbringing to instil a strong sense of community, so a sense of having grieved or injured the fellowship by one's sins comes much more readily. If the penitent individual is to experience a sense of *uhuru* (freedom), he will find a deep need to be 'in the light' with the whole body of the local church. Of course, such a movement brings its own dangers and temptations, especially of someone 'confessing' so overtly that others are harmed rather than edified. So church members are encouraged to apply the basic principle, 'let all things be done for edification'. No doubt the European Christian, with his strong inheritance of Graeco-Roman individualism, will be tempted to ask, 'Is this kind of thing really necessary?' A comparison of the vitality of East African Christianity today, compared to the situation in his own country, may persuade him that here, at least, he may have something to learn from fellow Christians elsewhere.[2]

However, we should perhaps temper this commendation with a further observation. There is an important truth in John Stott's assertion that 'confession must be made *to* the person *against* whom we have sinned and *from* whom we need and desire to receive forgiveness.'[3] He himself goes on to distinguish between sins against God alone which should be the subject of 'secret confession'; sins against other individuals, for 'private confession'; and sins against a whole fellowship group, for 'public confession'. We may need to be prepared, however, in the light of the theologizing in which we have just engaged, to broaden our concepts of who *is* injured by our sin. If we belong to a 'body', can we really suppose that *any* infection in one 'member' leaves the whole uninjured?

1 I am indebted to Martin Peppiatt, Vicar of St. Stephen's, East Twickenham, for help with this case-study.
2 For a brief account see W. B. Anderson *The Church in East Africa 1840-1974* (Central Tanganyika Press, P.O. Box 15, Dodoma, 1977, distributed by S.P.C.K. in England) e.g. pp.119, 124-5, 178.
3 *Confess Your Sins* (London 1964) p.12.

3. PASTORAL 'PENANCE'

The remainder of this booklet is taken up with the raising of a wide range of issues in, of necessity, extremely summary form, in the hope that the reader will be stimulated to think through for himself (perhaps with the aid of some of the further reading suggested) the ramifications of all that has been said so far. For the sake of some sort of order in the presentation of these issues we have distinguished between pastoral and liturgical matters (the 'Ministry' and 'Worship' of this series), but it should be particularly stressed that the two are (or at least, should be!) inextricably interwoven in practice. However it may be valid to make a distinction between the 'informal' and the 'formal' aspects of penance, though that in itself begs many questions. Indeed the question of just where one draws such a line may be crucial to one's basic attitude to the whole idea of penance. The neglect of this by many Christians lies in the fact that personal ministry in this area has become too much of a mere formality in some quarters! On the other hand I am indebted to my colleague, Father Austin Masters, of the Society of the Sacred Mission, for pointing out that there is a widely-held feeling among many anglo-catholics today that the very existence of 'private' confession and confessors is a tacit admission of the Church's failure to *be* the forgiving, reconciling community Christ meant it to be, (although there would need to be relatively small house-churches to sustain this ideal—a fact seemingly borne out by the East African experience just described, and by modern charismatic developments). The way that modern western society fobs off *medical* care of the elderly, the mentally ill, and the chronically sick onto 'professional' nurses is seen as a parallel example of a questionable modern propensity to 'leave it to the expert'. To this, one can only add that perhaps we need at present to accommodate this prevailing attitude to some extent, though at the same time seeking to move nearer to the ideal. One way that the evangelical will explore to this end, is to discourage too great a dependence on the *ordained* minister alone as a 'confessor', and to explore more fully the 'priesthood of *all* believers' in relation to the injunction 'confess your sins to one another' (Jas. 5.16).

The Modern Western Social Framework

It is important to recognize, in respect of contemporary pastoral ministry in this area, the prevailing philosophical fashions and the ruling sociological factors that predominate. It is the essential genius of Christianity, and part of its essential truth, that it is capable of appropriate adaptation and application to the *real* needs of every age and of every culture. In our society, for instance, existentialism has given rise to a great emphasis on the experiential; the so-called scientific world-view has sharpened the (imagined) 'divide' between the material and the immaterial elements of 'reality'; atheistic materialism undermines the imperatives of spiritual values; and agnostic humanism freely encourages the casual excuse 'it's only human' to condone attitudes that the Christian has traditionally regarded as *sub*-human! As a result modern man finds himself cut adrift from objective standards, confronted by apparently irreconcilable 'authorities', assailed by consumerism, and left to 'do his own thing'—a devalued individual isolated from any meaningful 'community', and denied a relevant spirituality.

Above all, the would-be pastor of the modern penitent has to come to terms with the all-pervasive influence of psychology—standing, as it so often does, at the confluence of science, humanism, a-theism and existentialism. Not that the Christian need take a wholly negative view of psychology. The Clinical Theology movement has done much to try and work out a viable synthesis here. (And for those who are worried about a possible conflict between Christianity and Psychology, in the area of our study, Max Thurian offers some valuable correctives.[1]) The insights of 'group therapy', for instance, highlight the importance of introducing a 'penitent' into a group (or church fellowship) situation at the appropriate time.[2] Or again, as Harry Williams has recently and very movingly testified[3], psychotherapy may even be God's chosen *means* of bringing a person to contrition and confession. But we must beware of expecting too much from this source. Psychology as an autonomous discipline is the product of a fallacious philosophical system which denies or ignores the essentially *unitive* view of man adopted by biblical Christianity, and therefore it has strict limitations for our purpose.[4] Nevertheless, along with the other modern influences noted, it does help us to identify certain areas of need in modern man which will predominate in our pastoral ministry to the penitent.

We may perhaps single out a need for 'acceptance'—'just as I am'[5]; a need for assurance that forgiveness *is* possible; a need to deal with overbearing feelings of *guilt* that persist[6]; a need to provide some effective 'check' against repetition of an habitual sin[7]; and a need sometimes to awaken dead consciences to unsuspected sources of profound disquiet, as particularly pressing features of our own contemporary culture.

Common Counselling Situations

There is space to do little more here than itemize some of the more frequent situations that the pastor comes across, where the process of contrition, confession, absolution and satisfaction will prove to be the chief 'means of

---

[1] See his chapter, 'Confession and Psychoanalysis' in *Confession* (ET, SCM, London, 1958) pp.78-99).
[2] In a recent conversation about the large number of apparent spiritual and emotional 'cripples' in a particular congregation, an older evangelical friend told me that it often used to be said, 'You can tell a live church by the number of *passengers* it is carrying!'
[3] In art., 'Psychotherapy as Repentance', in *Christian* Vol. 4. No. 2 (1977) pp.122-126.
[4] cf. Max Thurian *op. cit.* p.81 'The psychoanalyst limits himself to the discernment of the purely psychological causes of a state of disorder or neurosis. . . . This limitation of the domain of psychology, which is quite proper to it as a science, permits the Christian cure of the soul to be exercised alongside psychoanalysis, without competing or in any way being confused with it.'
[5] A particular *forte* of Samaritans and Marriage Guidance Counsellors.
[6] Thurian (*op. cit.* p.84) points out that a 'guilt-*complex*' is morbid and irrational, and should not be confused with *genuine* guilt. (One of the great sadnesses of the modern situation is the number of people who are going around for years burdened with an unnecessary load of guilt, just for lack of the right means of deliverance from it.) .
[7] The habit of making penance is itself a powerful check on sin. One is less inclined to sin when one knows one is going to have to 'make confession' if one does.

PENANCE

grace' for the one who is being helped. We may, however, distinguish three broad categories, namely those situations in which the person's relationship with *God* is primarily involved; those in which personal relationships with *others* are the predominant concern; and those which have more to do with the individual's *own* spiritual health and self-esteem.

In the first category, for instance, we would put the teenager who reveals a morbid fear of God's wrath against her, so that her whole existence is darkened by it; the dying old man whose wasted, careless life suddenly jumps out to condemn him; the demented woman who has compromised her (perhaps even mistaken) principles and entered into a 'forbidden' relationship with (say) a divorced man; the devoted Christian worker who once gave way to his curiosity and submitted to the God-forbidden blandishments of spiritist seances; and the respectable pillar of the local church who is beginning to discover just where his involvement in free-masonry is really leading him.

The second category would include the lonely widow who finds it impossible to forgive a wrong she feels she has suffered at the hands of a close relative (even though he has gone to her time and again to seek reconciliation); the couple whose marriage is clouded by a petty quarrel for which neither will admit any responsibility; and even the stubborn child who has been brought by his elder sister for arbitration in a seemingly intractable dispute over a small possession. (The simple childhood 'liturgies' of reconciliation are a most fruitful and formative field for the practice of penance).

As to the third, we might cite such familiar examples as the middle-aged man whose gambling or drinking is beginning to undermine his competence as a husband and father; the self-indulgent woman unable and unwilling to see any spiritual cause of her debilitating disease; the bereaved, self-vilified son overcome with remorse at his neglect of his suddenly-dead mother; and the would-be 'saint' wearied and discouraged by long years of struggling against the apparently irresistible urge to sexual self-indulgence.

Thus we particularize the pastor's involvement with the bereaved, the sick, the dying, the casualties of occult involvement, the bitter, the fearful, the spoilt, the weak-minded, the weak-willed, the habitual sinner and many, many more. The relevance of penance for each will be obvious. To lead them through it is the pastor's calling.

Some variable factors
Here, we simply share some thoughts on items of which the pastor needs to be aware in this context.

First, he needs to be sensitive to a great range of possibilities where *guilt* is concerned. He may encounter the quite inordinate self-vilification that typified certain forms of asceticism. At the other extreme he may find an almost total off-loading of guilt onto, say, a marriage partner or even an unclean spirit. And he may need to deal, in himself and others, with the

PASTORAL 'PENANCE'

sort of *corporate* sense of guilt that assailed Moses (Ex. 32.30ff.), Daniel (Dan. 9.3ff) and Ezra (Ezra (Ezra 9.5ff.), or even 'vicarious' guilt—an attempt to assume responsibility for the sins of others.[1]

The sins of family, church, nation and world[2] loom large in the consciousness of many. Or, on the other hand, he may be confronted with undue scrupulosity and 'perfectionism' where sin is concerned.[3]

Second, he will discover an enormous variation in people's *capacity* for penance. Jesus consistently pointed out, for instance, the correlation between our willingness to forgive others and the possibility of being ourselves forgiven. The formula of the Lord's Prayer in this respect is a powerful key in pastoral counselling. And the dreadful possibility of encountering hard-hearted *impenitence* is ever-present. The repetition of the history of the Pharaoh with whom Moses dealt (Ex. chs. 7-12) is an infrequent but by no means unknown occurrence.

And without penitence there can be no reconciliation, and formal acts of confession and absolution are worse than useless.[4]

Lastly he needs to discern in each case what will be the appropriate *context* for penance. For some this will be essentially a private, personal matter—or even a *secret* transaction between the person and God alone—though the pastor will be more concerned with giving advice as to what would be the most *edifying* context, rather than submitting uncritically to the penitent's own desires. Indeed one of the most needful but difficult tasks of the pastor may be to persuade the penitent that it would be more appropriate to make penance in the context of a small group or a public congregation.[5] But here we step over into the sphere of liturgical practice.

---

[1] I am told that this has been a constantly recurring theme in post-war Lutheran pastoral experience in Germany—where the enormous legacy of personal and corporate guilt engendered by Nazism is still not yet fully exorcized.

[2] It was in penance for the sins of the world that the flagellants underwent their atrocious ordeals.

[3] A frequent product, strange to say, of both monasticism *and* the 'Keswick' movement!

[4] It has been the writer's experience that *this* is the most frequent cause of failure in ineffective exorcisms, for instance.

[5] The minister also needs to be alert, on the other hand, for the occurrence *during* worship of quite spontaneous experiences of remorse and contrition. These are particularly likely at the communion rail and during funerals.

4. LITURGICAL 'PENANCE'

The provision that the Church makes liturgically for penance will be as varied as the situations just outlined require. We have chosen to systematize what follows in terms of regular provision, occasional provision and exceptional provision, but certain features appertain to all three, and these come first.

General Points

Logically we might begin with the subject of 'penitential introductions'. Should they be an invariable prelude to *all* acts of praise and worship? Should penitence not rather come as a response to the realization of God's holiness, as with Isaiah (Is. 6.1-5) and Peter (Lk. 5.1-8). In this case a verse of scripture and a hymn which invoke a sense of the holy will be a more appropriate introduction to worship.

Can there *be* such a thing as a *general* confession? Ought we not rather to recognize that this needs supplementing with a preliminary period of silence, when specific sins can be brought to the Lord and confessed, before (as with the new Roman Catholic rites) a united expression of contrition is made?

And what about postures and gestures? It may no longer be appropriate to adopt sackcloth and ashes, but one would feel that kneeling (rather than sitting or standing) was important. And, dare one say it, the simple devotional act of marking one's breast with the sign of the cross at the moment of absolution ought *not* to be despised![1]

Certain liturgical forms are intended specifically as aids and stimulants to confession. Are we always conscious of this, and careful to bring this out, in our use, for instance, of the Ten Commandments, the Lord's summary of the Law, or the Kyries?

Other forms in worship function themselves (or at least offer suitable form) as acts of confession. Do we make full and proper use of the penitential psalms, hymns like 'Dear Lord and Father of mankind', or the Lord's Prayer itself for this purpose?[2] The 'Gloria in Excelsis' also has a strong penitential aspect. For this reason it seems to some to be highly inappropriate in the place it occupies in the 1662 Communion Service.

Finally, what about General Absolutions? In the light of what has been said about the functions of the Church and the individual minister in this respect, is there really any case for maintaining the distinction between the 'performative' formula (reserved to the 'priest') and the 'declaratory' (assigned for the deacon or lay reader)?

---

[1] cf. the editorial of *New Blackfriars* for March 1977 (already cited): 'How we celebrate it [i.e. penance] sacramentally is not a matter of pre-requisites demanded by God before he will forgive us, it is a matter of signs and appropriate human gestures, a matter, amongst other things, of psychology and of the symbolic structures of our society.'

[2] Incidentally, some feel it is more appropriate to omit the 'ascription' at the end of the Lord's prayer when it is being used in the context of penance.

LITURGICAL 'PENANCE'

Regular Provision
So we come to a consideration of the specific liturgical opportunities that the Church provides for penance. We begin with those that recur regularly and are intended, (annually, weekly or daily) for *all* members of the new covenant.

(a) Annual
We have noted already in Judaism, Islam and Shinto the yearly pattern of *Yom Kippur, Ramadan* and *O-harai*. For the Christian the equivalent is Lent[1], the annual opportunity for self-discipline and self-discovery, modelled on the example of Jesus in his forty days preparation for his ministry.

The solemnities of Ash Wednesday, especially with the searching challenge of the Commination Service[2], provide a fitting start to the period of voluntarily undertaken self-denial[3] that culminates in the liturgical commemoration of the passion and death of Jesus, when the Good Friday services offer a momentous climax to what can be a most edifying annual exercise in personal penance. Perhaps the use of Renewal of Baptismal Vows would prolong this to the dawn of Easter.

(b) Weekly
By far the most important regular provision for penance is the weekly eucharist.[4] Some indeed view it as the culmination of the whole process of reconciliation.[5] We may not necessarily wish to go so far as that, but it is certain that there is in the New Testament the clearest possible connection between the two.[6]

The self-examination called for will involve both preparation *before,* and recollection *during,* the actual service. The first exhortation of the Prayer Book service envisages this primarily as a do-it-yourself exercise[7], though it leaves the way open to approach the Minister, if necessary, for counselling. It is a matter of regret that this whole element seems totally lacking from the revisions so far offered.

---

[1] Though the Methodist tradition of a Covenant (renewal) Service at the beginning of each New Year commends itself for wider consideration.

[2] Echoing, as its introduction reminds us, the 'godly discipline' in the primitive church when 'such persons as stood convicted of notorious sin were put to open penance.' But more modern forms are none the less welcome!

[3] Modern living affords ample opportunity for appropriate discipline here. The writer finds abstinence from television and home-made wine to be salutary. (Though his evangelical 'innocence' has taken some severe knocks at Church House when it comes to the amount of 'relief' that Catholic casuistry can offer during the fast!).

[4] We have argued the case elsewhere for a *weekly* eucharist, cf. *Anamnesis in the Eucharist* (Grove Liturgical Studies No. 5, March 1976) p.16.

[5] cf. J. D. Crichton, *op. cit.* p.29.

[6] The significance of Paul's exhortation in 1 Cor. 11.27-32 is incontrovertible. And cf. Matt. 5.23, 24. This suggests that liturgically it *is* appropriate to have penitence immediately before the Kiss of Peace, and related to access to the Table.

[7] There are many simple guides offered for methodical self-examination, though Martin Thornton, in *The Purple Headed Mountain* (London, 1962) pp.42ff., pertinently warns against superficial 'check-lists', and also argues strongly (p.41) that self-examination is a question of facing *facts* rather than stirring up *emotions*.

PENANCE

The point is also made, in the introductory rubric of the Prayer Book, that the eucharist is viewed (as in 1 Cor. 5.1ff, 2 Cor. 2.5ff., etc.), as a legitimate and important vehicle of church discipline, with 'ex-communication' as a means of bringing people to repentance; and as a holy service to be guarded against any 'open and notorious evil liver'. Surely the modern Church ought to be much more sensitive to the same possibilities and concerns?

As for the service itself, its whole pattern embodies the process of penance as we have described it, with evident opportunities for contrition and confession, absolution and satisfaction.[1] The treatment of the last aspect is particularly helpful, with a strong emphasis on the redeeming work of Christ *preceding* the self-oblation of the worshipper for a life of service in response to this. The place of the 'Peace' in the modern revisions, coming as it does straight after absolution, and giving immediate opportunity for any *personal* reconciliations, is an especially powerful focus for the *corporate* enjoyment of the fruits of penance, as the whole reconciled body moves forward to the climax of the sacrament.

(c) Daily

It has almost completely dropped from sight in most places, but the Church has, in Morning and Evening Prayer, *daily* offices which incorporate regular provision for penance. We need not dwell on this, though we may comment on the diminution of this element again in the modern revisions of these offices. But some might see a strong case for the widespread revival of their daily use in their Old Testament antecedents—the Morning and Evening sacrifice (Ex. 29.38-46). The way that these *daily* offices have so often displaced the weekly eucharist on Sundays (and still continue to do so), should however, be a profound source of disquiet to biblical Christians!

Occasional Provision

Provision is also made for penance at certain occasions in the life of the believer which, though not regular, will arise at some time or other for most. These will frequently have a more individual significance than the Church's regular liturgical provision allows. Occasions of initiation, for instance, at *baptism* or *confirmation* have a vital penitential element, when the new member (or his sponsors) have opportunity publicly to acknowledge that sin which gives point to the whole transaction that lies at the heart of the New Covenant. And this also has a residual significance. Martin Luther, for instance, testified that he found one of the most effective answers to the Tempter was, 'I have been baptized'. To be able to point even a young child to this 'means of grace' is a sometimes neglected argument in the controversies over pedobaptism.

---

[1] Warren Tanghe, in a review of Nicholas Sagovsky's Grove booklet in *Faith and Unity* Vol. XXI, No. 1 (1977) p.23, argues for 'confession' as the beginning of the whole rite, as in the new Mass, on the grounds that 'both the Liturgy of the Word and the Liturgy of the Sacrament are encounters with the Living Christ, and thus equally require penitential preparation.' We are not convinced that the case for such a *sacramental* view of the Liturgy of the Word has yet been satisfactorily made. It does seem surprisingly Barthian as an explanation of current Roman practice!

LITURGICAL 'PENANCE'

The connection between penance and *weddings* is not so obvious, but it is nevertheless there. In the service the solemn exhortation, the Lord's Prayer and the intercessions all allude to aspects of it. It looms larger, as one would expect, in any blessing of a 'civil' marriage, or in any provision for the remarriage of divorced persons. And certainly in *preparing* a couple for marriage the pastor will do his best to lay sound foundations for those penitential practices which will prove so vital to a successful lifelong partnership.

The penitential elements of the *funeral* service are more widely recognized, though not without some controversy. The traditional psalms, the prayer at the graveside, (again) the Lord's Prayer, and the final intercessions of the 1662 service all clearly incorporate this. The importance for the bereaved of opportunity to express their penitence has already been pleaded, and it is a great loss pastorally that this aspect is so sweepingly 'toned down' in the Series 3 revision.

Exceptional Provision

Finally, for the sake of completeness, a few words may be said about those liturgical opportunities provided for circumstances which may be described as 'out of the ordinary'.

Perhaps the provision of liturgical penance for the *sick* and the *dying* might seem more properly to belong to the previous section, but we would argue that the most significant difference is that they are much more rarely used in Anglican tradition, and that they are, unlike the *occasional* offices, rarely conducted publicly.[1] Furthermore, it has been the writer's own experience that the 'ad hoc' use of certain psalms and *extempore* prayers has seemed more appropriate to this need[2], and even the singing of certain well-loved hymns has proved its worth. It should perhaps be mentioned in passing that the service for the Visitation of the Sick in the Book of Common Prayer furnishes the clearest example, in Church of England provisions, for the practice of confession of sin in the presence of another person. Whether it is 'auricular' is not quite so clear. The indicative first person absolution is the most 'exceptional' feature of the rite—presumably for a situation where cutting corners is pastorally necessary.

The ministry of *healing* and of *exorcism*, as has been mentioned already, are intimately and inextricably bound up with the whole sphere of penance, and the provision for adequate liturgical expression for this is of paramount importance. Because of the 'charismatic' nature of such ministry a strong case can be made out for the loosest possible 'form of service', but the following of some sort of liturgical *framework,* at least, which embodies adequate opportunity for confession and absolution seems highly desirable, to say the least.

[1] An even more 'borderline' case is the service provided for Thanksgiving of Women after Child-birth. The writer strongly demurs from the view that this service is now obsolete and that therefore its revision is unnecessary. However, the Thanksgiving For the Birth of a Child may fill the need—though hardly a penitential one.

[2] Though, on one memorable occasion, it was the repetition of the once familiar General Confession that brought peace with God to a dying old man who had long ago wandered away from the Church.

PENANCE

Any moves to bring about the re-unification of churches in the present ecumenical climate will eventually raise the question of *Services of Reconciliation.* The element of penance incorporated in any proposed service will be a most accurate touchstone of the true underlying attitudes of the Covenanting parties. And any suspicion of (say) concealed episcopalian triumphalism on such an occasion would become quickly evident by such a test!

In conclusion, we may perhaps make some reference to the possibility of *acts of public penitence.* When one considers the waste, the materialism, the economic exploitation, the racialism, the environmental pollution, the 'Hiroshimas', the 'Dresdens', and the 'Belsens' of twentieth-century life, one can see ample material for such events. It is our feeling, however, that whilst the *Church* may properly express its penitence, in solidarity with the human community, for such things[1], it is not theologically sound to look for the same sort of thing from a nation. We are very sceptical, therefore, of the propriety or efficacy of urging acts of *national* penitence of this kind.[2]

---

[1] The recent Festival of Light rally in Trafalgar Square contained a most moving example of this.
[2] This was felt to be a major weakness for instance of the musical presentation 'If my people . . .' The New Testament people of God are not at liberty to apply the tenets of theocratic Israel to their own secular states.

5. 'MATTERS ARISING'

In conclusion, the following observations are offered in the hope that they will take the reader further in the area covered by this booklet. We see possibilities for action in personal life, in the corporate life of the local church, and by official action at the centre.

For Personal Action

Our main conviction, born of personal experience, is that many Christians have thrown out the baby with the bathwater where the considered and methodical *personal practice of penance* is concerned. One sees the danger of penance, like fasting or even prayer, becoming a mechanical routine rather than a 'means of grace' for particular needs. But, surely, its neglect (especially in the light of unanimous biblical, Catholic, Orthodox, Reformation, Puritan, Methodist and Tractarian teaching) is one of the main reasons why so many are robbed of the 'joy of salvation' and the spontaneity of praise which is the hall-mark of the truly penitent. If anyone is looking for a *starting-point* in today's world perhaps the mention of materialistic lifestyles, waste, personal indulgence, spiritual indifference, lax morality, indolent television viewing, or the isolation of elderly parents may provide it. And to any who are still not wholly convinced, and to those who would like to know more, may we commend the following *books,* which give a much fuller treatment:

J. D. Crichton: *The Ministry of Reconciliation* (Chapman, London, 1974).
John Gunstone: *The Liturgy of Penance* (Faith Press, London, 1966).
Kenneth Ross: *Hearing Confessions* (SPCK, London, 1974).
Nicholas Sagovsky: *Modern Roman Catholic Worship—Baptism and Penance* (Grove Booklet No. 43, 1976).
Basilea Schlink: *Repentance—the Joy-filled Life* (Lakeland, London, 1969).
J. R. W. Stott: *Confess Your Sins* (Hodder, London, 1964).
Martin Thornton: *The Purple-Headed Mountain* (Faith, London, 1962).
Max Thurian: *Confession* (SCM, London, 1958).

For Corporate Action

In the local church the first need may well be for conscious *acceptance and expectation* on the part of all for the process of penance outlined, and adequate provision for it. The reinstatement of the central importance of a main *weekly eucharist* would be a first priority in this respect. The development of *home groups* as units for the practice of penance (among other things) could be another edifying move in the right direction. And, although the possibility of 'conversion' without overt repentance should be recognized, the rehabilitation of a call to repentance in the work of *evangelism* could profitably be the subject of a course of congregational study, and for subsequent implementation. This may be especially relevant for outreach to the *real* outsider (in contrast to those with some residual Christianity who are the more usual objects of local mission!).

PENANCE

For Official Action

At least two lines of response to the matter of this booklet on the part of the leadership of the Church suggest themselves. In the first place, and in keeping with the introductory rubric to the Prayer Book Communion Service, a revival of the *episcopal* discipline of *'putting out'* and *'restoring'* the impenitent and the penitent respectively might be called for. One would hope that the necessity actually to exercise this would be relatively infrequent, but its apparent total desuetude today cannot help but contribute to the great laxity in the Church which we have been decrying. In the second place, and finally, would it not be proper to call upon the *Liturgical Commission* to take the whole process of penance much more into account in their work? In particular might one ask for modern exhortations for the eucharist; a revised form of the Commination Service for Ash Wednesday; the re-instatement of the penitential elements in the funeral service; and the consideration of the provision (for those who feel they need it) of a simple liturgical form for *individual* confession and absolution (perhaps along the lines of that in the new South African Prayer Book).